Twenty Sumr
in English La

Twenty Summaries in English Language for GCE

Brian Rowe BA
Senior Lecturer in English
Maria Assumpta College of Education
London W8

R. A. Banks MA PhD
Head of the Department of English
West London Institute of Higher Education
Borough Road, Isleworth, Middlesex

HODDER AND STOUGHTON
LONDON SYDNEY AUCKLAND TORONTO

ISBN 0 340 18597 X

Eleventh impression 1985

Typesetting by Thomson Litho Ltd, East Kilbride
Printed and bound in Great Britain for
Hodder and Stoughton Educational,
a division of Hodder and Stoughton Ltd,
Mill Road, Dunton Green, Sevenoaks, Kent
by St Edmundsbury Press, Bury St Edmunds, Suffolk.

INTRODUCTION

Summarising a story, the plot of a film, a speech, a newspaper account, someone else's views, or a report is a skill which we all need to use at one time or another in our lives. This skill depends essentially on comprehension and selection—the ability to see and choose what is important or what is relevant and to re-arrange it in a shorter, more readily understood form. Inevitably the summary will reflect the perceptiveness of the person making it and his control in isolating and setting out ideas and facts according to some pre-determined criteria laid down. In GCE examinations, for example, candidates are told what facts or groups of ideas they are expected to extract from a passage and how they should re-present them—how many words they should use as a maximum, what paragraphing to introduce, and how far they should reproduce words and phrases from the original.

The summary is essentially different from précis. In examinations set during the fifties and early sixties candidates were expected to read a passage carefully and then to make a précis by reducing it to about one-third of its former length. Often this meant to some that repetitive phrases, figurative language, and verbose expressions should be removed, irrespective of the style of the writer, and the mutilated remains were to be paraphrased into a whole. The unwary and the weak relied heavily on a 'scissors-and-paste' technique and often produced garbled and meaningless work; the strong-minded, but ill-advised, resorted to free composition. Examiners, too, had their problems, as they were faced with the very doubtful task of presenting for the attention of intelligent candidates passages which were perhaps suitable for précis but which were badly-written or passages which were well-written but which quietly and obstinately refused to submit to mutilation.

The new summarising exercises in GCE examinations, however, do not require candidates to reduce the whole sense of a passage to about one-third of its original length. They are asked to select relevant material from a well-written extract and, ignoring all other information, to re-assemble this material in good, consecutive, coherent prose. It is essentially an exercise which demands understanding, discrimination, skill in ordering ideas, and a good prose style.

With these requirements in mind we suggest, therefore, the following approach to GCE summary work which will help candidates to gain experience and develop their skill.

1 First read the passage quickly to establish its fundamental approaches, arguments, and development. Then re-read it carefully and thoroughly, looking closely at the details, until you have understood it as fully as you can.

2 Examine and decide from the introductory instructions *exactly* what you

are required to look for in the passage and what information you are expected to select.

3 Read the passage again and choose relevant material, wherever it occurs. This is best set out in rough notes as you work through the passage. Group the ideas and arrange the material under paragraph headings determined from the instructions. Use your own words and phrases as much as possible.

4 Go through the passage once more to ensure that *all* the relevant material has been extracted and summarised in your notes under the correct heading.

5 Make sure that your notes are in your own words *so far as is possible.* Sometimes it is not possible to rephrase the wording of the passage economically and then it is perfectly acceptable to use some short phrases from the extract itself.

6 Write out the notes in rough paragraphs *without referring to the original* while you are doing so in order to avoid the temptation of using the words and phrasing of the passage.

7 Count the words you have used in your 'rough' summary and amend your work to bring it into line with the number of words required.

8 Write out your 'fair copy' of the summary and cross through any notes, leaving them still legible, however. (Credit will often be given for this work if you run out of time and cannot finish the summary.)

9 Re-read your work to make sure that your spelling and punctuation are correct.

10 Place at the end the number of words you have used. (Examiners will assess the number of words you have actually used.)

This methodical approach to writing a summary will ensure that the material is carefully considered and evaluated. The ultimate quality of the work, however, will depend on a candidate's fundamental and acquired abilities to read, understand, think, and present his ideas clearly in well-ordered prose.

B.R.
R.A.B.

SUMMARY ONE

The following passage is taken from an article on comics.

Using only the information given in the passage, write a summary consisting of *two* paragraphs:

a what the chief characteristics of English comics are, *and*

b why these characteristics appeal to children

Do not try to summarise everything in the passage, but select from it the material needed for your paragraphs. These should be written in clear, concise English, *and as far as possible in your own words,* although you may retain some words and brief expressions which cannot be accurately or economically replaced.

Your whole summary should not exceed 150 words altogether, and at the end you must state the number of words used.

To understand the appeal of comics you have to become a 10-year-old addict again; to summon up the time when every bristle on Desperate Dan's chin seemed precious, every exploit of Korky the Cat irresistible. Comics are enjoyed like the favourite games which a child is content to repeat over and over again. Clearly they satisfy a permanent need. As one would expect, the most violent slapstick tends to be directed against figures of authority—which for children means every adult to some extent, but particularly parents and teachers. No gags are more popular than the ones in which 'Sir' is humiliated. An unending procession of teachers (they wear their mortar-boards at all times) are regularly charged by bulls, butted by goats, presented with cakes made out of plaster of paris, and assailed with blunt instruments. But the violence works both ways. As often as not the pupils come off worse than the master, or the last frame of a story will show an irate parent about to exact revenge. There is an ambivalent attitude, too, towards low cunning: it is often held up for admiration, but the habitual tricksters usually come to grief.

The humour of the comics depends on the assumption that children are in a perpetual state of war, both with their seniors and with one another. The presiding spirit, 100 per cent anti-genteel, is that of the Bash Street Kids in 'The Beano'. Anyone who still thinks of childhood as the age of innocence should consider how unsentimental children are about themselves. They seem perfectly happy to be depicted in the comics as thorough-going brats. Yet, comics constantly remind one how aggressive children are, but at the same time how defenceless they can be. (The playground bully, for instance, is a recurrent villain.)

Second only to violence as a theme for fantasy is magic. A long line of schoolboy heroes have been equipped with supernatural powers, from Sammy and his Magic Wishbone (now defunct) to Peter the Piper, who only has to play his pipes in order to bring statues to life. If magic provides a consolation for the weak, a means of catching up with and overtaking adults, it also offers a retreat to early childhood.

American picture-books—the worst ones, that is—are the only case I know where 'comic' is equated with outright malevolence. The cruelty has come out from behind the humour and utterly swamped it. In crime-comics the drawings are detailed and realistic; in the British children's variety they are so primitive that they can scarcely even be called caricatures—they are simply pictographs which help to tell the story. If they were slicker, they would lose their flavour, the innocent crudeness that is part of their basic appeal.

Meanwhile comics are frowned on by headmasters, confiscated, read furtively under the desk-lid. And this is as it should be: adult disapproval is part of the game, a kind of guarantee of authenticity. In the eyes of children it confirms that they are reading something subversive, escaping to a world where the pressures from above no longer operate. Like all true humour, what the comics hold out is first and foremost the promise of freedom.

SUMMARY TWO

The following passage is taken from an account of the last days of the composer Mozart.

Using only the information given in the passage, write a summary consisting of *two* paragraphs:

a the suspicious and unusual circumstances surrounding Mozart's death, *and*

b the reasons why Mozart might have been murdered

Do not try to summarise everything in the passage, but select from it the material needed for your paragraphs. These should be written in clear, concise English, *and as far as possible in your own words,* although you may retain some words and brief expressions which cannot be accurately or economically replaced.

Your whole summary should not exceed 150 words altogether, and at the end you must state the number of words used.

A few months before Mozart died, in 1791, he told his wife, Constanze: 'I shall not last much longer. I am convinced that I have been poisoned.'

Poison was a recognised political weapon of the time. Mozart believed he was being poisoned with *aqua toffana.* This toxin, well known in eighteenth-century poisoning circles, was undetectable in small doses, and produced results only after a convenient lapse of time.

Mozart had made enemies in his lifetime. He had publicly rejected his former employer, the Prince Archbishop Colloredo, claiming that he was treated no better than a servant, when everybody knew this was what a musician was supposed to be. Moreover, he had succeeded in staging a brilliant operatic version of Beaumarchais' revolutionary comedy, *The Marriage of Figaro.* This play, harmless enough to us, was banned by the Viennese authorities for its alleged revolutionary message.

After Mozart's death the conduct of several people, if not exactly sinister, certainly called for explanation. The burial arrangements were undertaken by a wealthy friend, Baron von Swieten. He promptly had the widow removed from the premises and ordered the cheapest possible funeral.

The cemetery, belonging to the church of St Marx, lay outside the city walls and only a small group of friends assembled at the cathedral. The party did not accompany the body to the grave, but turned back at the city gates: the weather, they consistently maintained afterwards, was too bad—rain and snow. According to the records of the Vienna Observatory, however, the weather was calm, and rather pleasant throughout. In addition, the grave was not marked by a cross, though even in a third-class funeral like Mozart's such a sign would have been normal procedure. By the following day, thanks also to a switch in grave-diggers, it was quite impossible to say where the body lay. Constanze did not even visit the cemetery for several years, and later claimed that the responsibility for a headstone was not hers, but that of the local council.

If Mozart was poisoned, it would scarcely have been extraordinary. Vienna in the eighteenth-century was an uncomfortable place. Intrigue, murder and real fear of revolution created a frantic atmosphere in the extravagant centre of the Habsburg empire. Perhaps the most damning thing of all for Mozart was that he was a very good composer. Antonio Salieri, the court musician, was envious of Mozart's obvious superiority as a composer, while Mozart in turn resented Salieri's influence and position. Though six years Mozart's senior, Salieri outlived him by many years. He is reported to have confessed to Mozart's murder, but this was dismissed as the ramblings of a senile mind, as Salieri was seventy-five when he made it and in a lunatic asylum. It is, however, rumoured to exist in writing and to be hidden in a church in Vienna.

SUMMARY THREE

The following passage is taken from an article on the arrival of a new child in a family.

Using only the information given in the passage, write a summary consisting of *two* paragraphs:

a how an older child reacts to having a new baby brother or sister, *and*

b what parents can do to help overcome the problems that arise for their older children with the arrival of a new baby in the family

Do not try to summarise everything in the passage, but select from it the material needed for your paragraphs. These should be written in clear, concise English, *and as far as possible in your own words,* although you may retain some words and brief expressions which cannot be accurately or economically replaced.

Your whole summary should not exceed 160 words altogether, and at the end you must state the number of words used.

A first-born child will have had the mother's complete attention. She is the supplier of all his needs and he will have been totally dependent on her. A second child will drastically alter the relationship. He will, in his turn, be completely demanding and the attention the first receives must decrease. He is bound to hate the new child for depriving him, and his mother for rebuffing him.

There are very many points in a child's development where he will be especially sensitive. At the age of two, as a child psychotherapist has shown, the child needs more physical contact with his mother than at one or three. A new arrival will frustrate this need. 'Then at three', says Dr Anderson, 'a girl will want most to be with her father. If he now seems to ignore her it will be a very bitter blow.' At five there is the gigantic emotional leap of starting school. 'Children are particularly vulnerable throughout their first five or six years', says Dr Dorothy Gibbs. 'It's only once the child is really established at school that the problems created by the arrival of a brother or sister are likely to diminish.'

The second child will naturally have feelings of rivalry towards the first, though these will be less ambivalent, as the older child will be as much a permanent fixture as his parents. The rivalry will develop as the two compete for the same kind of attention. As further children are born the patterns of rivalry will become complex. The first child may see the second as his rival; but the second may not reciprocate.

If a child of two snatches his baby sister's doll from her pram, demonstrate, by behaving affectionately, that you understand his feelings—put your arm round him as you steer him back to the pram and tell him he can play with the doll when the baby has finished with it. At this stage the older child often regresses, copying the behaviour which appears to him to be gaining the younger child approval and attention—such as crawling when he can walk quite well, or seeking help in dressing although he has learnt to do it by himself. Being naughty is another ploy children discover gains attention.

As the child grows older he may become afraid to learn because he is frightened his parents love only immature children. In this way, too, he may win more attention for himself and the learning block may become fixed, even after the threat itself has diminished.

If you find the older child attacking the younger, stop him—but tell him, explicitly, if he is old enough, that you understand how he feels. Do not insist that the older child is the only one to make concessions. Try to show him that being the older child has its own important advantages.

Of course, children do fight and hit each other and in itself this should not be alarming. This is not to say that violence should be allowed but you should acknowledge that your children have feelings and try to avoid situations which lead to direct conflicts between them.

SUMMARY FOUR

The following passage is taken from an article about flu viruses.

Using only the information given in the passage, write a summary consisting of *three* paragraphs:

a how viruses infect people, *and*

b how viruses change their natures, *and*

c how viruses are combated

Do not try to summarise everything in the passage, but select from it the material needed for your paragraphs. These should be written in clear, concise English, *and as far as possible in your own words*, although you may retain some words and brief expressions which cannot be accurately or economically replaced.

Your whole summary should not exceed 150 words altogether, and at the end you must state the number of words used.

Viruses have a difficult enough life, even without the new, better vaccine now being developed by the Medical Research Council.

Viruses live by infection. A virus attacks a living cell (flu attacks the cells lining our breathing apparatus) and takes it over. The genes in the cell's nucleus would normally be directing it to make new cells; but when the virus's genes take over, the cell starts instead to make new viruses. It can go on doing this until the cell bursts, spilling viruses out to infect other cells. But the process of infection is not easy. In the flu virus, the genes take the form of a spiral so delicate that exposure to the air would destroy it. Viruses have a protective shell of protein, part of whose task is to attach itself to a cell and pierce it to let the virus in. But the protein also mobilises the body's defences. These normally win, and the body is not infected.

The virus has further problems. Whether the body is successfully infected or not, its defences, once roused, stay roused for some time. With flu, as with other diseases, such as measles, the resistance—the immunity—lasts for years. The flu virus does have an answer to that—it changes its coat. Normally, the body identifies cells as invaders and then develops a specific form of attack; and it has to restart this process when the virus changes. The flu virus changes fairly radically every ten years or so and when it does, it finds the entire human race unprotected by resistance and available again as hosts.

The great problem in dealing with an epidemic is knowing, in advance, that you are going to have one. The strain has to be identified and then watched, and someone has to decide if an epidemic looks likely. The decision has to be made soon enough for the drug companies to rear enough viruses to be ready for the demand for vaccine. Because the immunity takes some time to develop, timing is crucial. The World Health Organisation plots the steady advance of each new flu strain and warns hospitals and drug companies. Records were fully started only in 1933, when a variety called A_0 swept through Europe. The next major change was in 1947—virus A_1; 1957 saw A_2, and 1968 a variety that was called Hongkong Flu.

Since records were started, these changes have always originated in Asia and worked their way north, as person infected person, to reach Europe and North America. The reasons for this pattern are not clear. If it is merely a question of the flu virus changing with time, there is no obvious reason why such a change should occur only in Asia.

There is another intriguing possibility. The genes in the flu virus are loosely connected. This means that when different strains of virus are close together, the pieces of virus can fairly easily become mixed up. Animals also suffer from flu, and there is a theory that in peasant communities, where people live in close contact with their animals, there is more opportunity for viruses to meet for a spot of gene-swapping.

These changes make it much more difficult to attack the disease. Virus infections cannot usually be treated with drugs or antibiotics: anything that would attack the infection would also attack the host's living cells, because the virus uses the cell's mechanism to multiply itself.

Virus diseases are best stopped before they infect, and the technique used is that of vaccination. For this, you collect some virus from a patient, rear it in a living creature, extract it, and then maltreat it so that it loses its ability to cause the disease you are trying to prevent, and this vaccine can then be used for injections.

SUMMARY FIVE

The following passage is taken from a discussion about the value of foreign travel.

Using only the information given in the passage, write a summary consisting of *two* paragraphs:

a the benefits offered to everyone by foreign travel, *and*

b the difficulties which can be caused by foreign travel

Do not try to summarise everything in the passage, but select from it the material needed for your paragraphs. These should be written in clear, concise English, *and as far as possible in your own words,* although you may retain some words and brief expressions which cannot be accurately or economically replaced.

Your whole summary should not exceed 160 words altogether, and at the end you must state the number of words used.

Every summer Europeans by the million climb on board flying boxes to exchange their little boxes by the city for little boxes by the sea in another country. Innocents abroad, they go armed with a simple faith that they will enjoy themselves and feel better afterwards. Some are armed also with a determined belief in cultural self-improvement. They go to satisfy their curiosity, their sense of adventure, the need for a rest, their determination to keep up with the Joneses.

In the sixties and early seventies armies of itinerant youth—pseudo hippies and authentic drop-outs alike—sparked local envy of their freedom along with a real concern for their morals and fear for farm produce and hygiene alike. For the millions, however, the consuming desire was to lie in the burning sun, to have drinks served as they stretched out in their leisure, to live like those from a higher social class, and make the beach the focal point of their lives. Inland throughout Europe and North Africa there are millions of square miles with sun, scenery, and water for swimming where the tourist armies can be absorbed, but the tourist seeks his suntan which proves he went abroad only on the beach and for this reason the finest coastlines and oldest cultures are degraded.

Never before has there been this constant, mass migration on such a scale as now. Millions of ordinary people with infinitely varied backgrounds are coming into prolonged contact with each other. This can promote—as perhaps can nothing else—the understanding between nations that can lessen the chance of war. It can generate respect in people of one country for the culture of another. It can bring swift prosperity to impoverished peoples and it can open the eyes of those in host countries where there are corruption and oppression. Art can be revitalized and dying crafts can be given a new lease of life. Palaces, cathedrals, and historical monuments in danger of falling to the ground can be looked after and preserved. Perhaps the biggest prospect offered is the release for the traveller from his own brand of tedium—the machine-dominated monotony of his own industrial society. He can run from the rain, and the sick and the weary can then be restored.

In reality, however, tourism's power is a two-edged sword. As things now stand the tourist is lucky to see anything more than his hotel, the pool, gift shops, and discothèques. Even the waiters are probably imported. The local poor profit hardly at all; they are given menial tasks with little dignity. Cynicism and disillusion set in and they begin to exploit each other. In the new economy prices rise and inflation sets in. Local stores find themselves competing with supermarkets; streets, once safe and quiet, are filled with cars and mopeds. The pace of life speeds up and the old entertainment enjoyed by local people gives way to tourist entertainment. Even churches and cathedrals become museums and bazaars. Craftsmanship is debased; for example, cheap imitations of fine Toledo metalwork degrade the centuries-old craft of proud artisans.

SUMMARY SIX

The following passage is taken from a passage pleading for better play facilities for city children.

Using only the information given in the passage, write a summary consisting of *two* paragraphs:

a the reasons why city children find playing games in the street difficult, *and*

b the ways in which children can find their amusement today

Do not try to summarise everything in the passage, but select from it the material needed for your paragraphs. These should be written in clear, concise English, *and as far as possible in your own words,* although you may retain some words and brief expressions which cannot be accurately or economically replaced.

Your whole summary should not exceed 130 words altogether, and at the end you must state the number of words used.

As a boy I used to live in a fascinating corner of a big city. There was a common opposite and a stable down the road where horses were kept; and lots of yards and alleyways. Modern building regulations do not allow for alleyways but the cars used not to trouble us much; indeed it used to be fun dodging them as they came round the corner sending us scuttling into the safety of our alley.

Now whole areas have been flattened and homes replaced by tall blocks of flats which, with few exceptions, merely add to the feeling of anonymity, have no provisions for a child's play, and effectively cut him off from contact with his fellows.

Children are especially victimised in modern cities. Traffic has swept away most of the old street games—hopscotch, marbles in the gutter, bowling hoops, spinning tops—and has made cycling a dangerous activity. The television set ensures that they will prefer to lead lonely, passive lives in their high-rise flats. The affluent society provides them with books, comics, and games, all ready-made, so that there is no real need to descend in a lift or run down flights of steps to meet the gang inventing its own spontaneous play in the streets.

Closing streets to traffic may help but as the child grows older he needs something more adventurous. It has been shown that children do not play in playgrounds for more than a tiny proportion—say five per cent—of their waking hours even if such places are provided. The rest of the time they are in the streets, the shops, at home, or a hundred and one other places.

All children are to some extent rebels against order and organisation.

They like to feel they are making their own fun. There is a world of difference between chancing on an old derelict house and having one put in front of them for the purpose. Nevertheless, adventure playgrounds do allow children to use their imaginations in creating their own play worlds.

Money spent on providing adequate playing facilities is not only an investment for the future but an insurance against the abundant energies of the young being used in less constructive ways. Some measures would cost very little—making school gymnasia and playing fields available outside school hours and during the holidays, for instance. Even an old church hall, no longer required for services, but still standing as a silent witness to an earlier community spirit can find new life as a discothèque or a meeting place for those helping the aged in voluntary work.

SUMMARY SEVEN

The following passage is taken from a report on old people's attitudes to clubs organised for them.

Using only the information given in the passage, write a summary consisting of *two* paragraphs:

a the attraction of clubs for old people, *and*

b the reasons why some old people do not go to clubs

Do not try to summarise everything in the passage, but select from it the material needed for your paragraphs. These should be written in clear, concise English, *and as far as possible in your own words,* although you may retain some words and brief expressions which cannot be accurately or economically replaced.

Your whole summary should not exceed 160 words altogether, and at the end you must state the number of words used.

Almost all the old people questioned said that they had talked and had a cup of tea at the last club meeting. A third had played bingo. A few had had a 'sing-song' or had seen some kind of entertainment, such as an advertising film or a show by a visiting musician or a group of amateur actors. One old woman said that she had listened to a Civil Defence lecture on what precautions to take against atomic fall-out.

Few old people report sitting by themselves in the club but very few went along by themselves in the first instance.

'It's always the same gang going on the outings. They've never come to me with an invitation to their club. Some people are just hangers-on. Yes, I might go if they asked me.'
Man, aged 74, Harrow

The need to feel wanted and part of a group is strong. Asked what they get out of going to old people's clubs the members are fairly unanimous:

'Good companionship. Somewhere to go.'

'We get together and have a good laugh.'

'Takes you out when you might not bother.'

'Just the company.'

Four-fifths mentioned one or more people they knew well at the club; nearly half were either sisters or neighbours. The majority of club members always sit with the same group.

About twelve per cent of the socially isolated have never been club members but say that they would be interested in attending if they were encouraged to go, if they had a friend, or if they received an invitation:

'I haven't bothered. If I had a friend I might go. Some of these clubs are just cliques.'
Woman, aged 68, Oldham

Others were explicitly troubled by what seems to be the passive role of clubs or their working-class atmosphere. They are too proud to join in:

'The local Darby and Joan's just for marrying them off. I can't picture myself sitting on a hard chair, wearing a funny hat and singing *Knees Up, Mother Brown*. They don't do anything. They ought to be marching up to London and making demands.'
Single woman, aged 65, Barnet

Ten per cent of those isolated from society had been to the old people's club near their home the week before the survey, but some said that increasing physical difficulty in getting there and back had made their visits rare. One man just stopped going altogether when his wife died—he just withdrew into himself through grief and loneliness.

The clubs are usually well organised. Christmas parties, outings to other old people's clubs, summer holidays out-of-season (May or September), or day-trips to the seaside allow the old to escape from their daily surroundings into an atmosphere where they can relive their past lives, talk with their contemporaries, and forget or revel in their aches and pains. Such activities are heavily subsidised and do not eat into the slight retirement pension most receive.

SUMMARY EIGHT

The following passage is taken from a commentary on the behaviour of teenagers.

Using only the information given in the passage, write a summary consisting of *two* paragraphs:

a the reasons for the growing independence of adolescents, *and*

b the effects of this independence on their behaviour

Do not try to summarise everything in the passage, but select from it the material needed for your paragraphs. These should be written in clear, concise English, *and as far as possible in your own words,* although you may retain some words and brief expressions which cannot be accurately or economically replaced.

Your whole summary should not exceed 160 words altogether, and at the end you must state the number of words used.

Young people now stay on at school till they are much older; one can hardly call a fifteen-year-old a child any more. Young people are also bigger and more physically mature than ever before. They are better educated and are encouraged to develop their own opinions since society no longer believes that tradition and old age are the main sources of wisdom.

Perhaps the decisive factor which has led society to distinguish older from younger children has been the new wealth and economic power which teenagers have enjoyed since the 1950s. In 1938 the average youth earned the equivalent of £1.30 a week and the average girl 90p. By the 1950s the earnings of teenagers had increased in value by fifty per cent and their spending capacity had doubled. Adult wages rose only half as fast. In the year 1964–5 teenagers between 15 and 21 spent £900 million and they contributed a quarter of the total amount spent by the country on consumer goods. Many young people still at school did part-time jobs, such as shop assistants, delivering newspapers or groceries and many received and expected good pocket money from their parents.

The image of teenagers as a special group was fostered by advertising, as consumer industries sought to sell a vast new range of goods especially for young people. Moreover, teenagers' wealth has given them the chance to follow their own fashions in clothes, music, and entertainment and thus emphasise the distinction between themselves and other age-groups.

The first signs of adolescent fashions appeared in the late 1940s with the popularity of the wide-shouldered jackets of the 'spiv' suit and the craze among a large minority for jiving and jazz clubs. The 'Teddy Boys' followed with their long hair, drainpipe trousers, velvet cuffs and collars, bootlace ties, and thick crêpe-soled shoes. Though a minority they had the power to represent, in its most extreme form, the general mood of teenage rebellion against the attitudes of adult society. More commonly, this rebellion made itself felt in many homes with arguments about dress, boy-friends, and late nights as parents naturally showed reluctance to relinquish the complete authority over their children that they had so far enjoyed.

In spite of the new freedom some adolescent amusements and pastimes barely changed. Comics remained popular with youngsters of all ages and voluntary service movements to help the aged, the sick and the homeless continued.

No longer are the young called up for national service but they can plan their careers without thought of interruption and can even spend time trying out jobs until they find what they are looking for. It is surprising, perhaps, that they are still slaves to their own fashion cults and distinctive groups still emerge with their own 'uniforms'. 1968 was the age of the flower children with their bells, beads, and psychedelic music. A year later the skinheads marched to war against the 'greasers' and the 'hippies'.

SUMMARY NINE

The following passage is taken from a history of the American Mid-West.

Using only the information given in the passage, write a summary consisting of *two* paragraphs:

a the reasons why the American Mid-West was opened up between 1855 and 1876, *and*

b the reasons for the violence of the period 1855–76 in the American Mid-West

Do not try to summarise everything in the passage, but select from it the material needed for your paragraphs. These should be written in clear, concise English, *and as far as possible in your own words,* although you may retain some words and brief expressions which cannot be accurately or economically replaced.

Your whole summary should not exceed 160 words altogether, and at the end you must state the number of words used.

The linking of New York with Chicago by rail in 1855, and St Louis with Kansas City the following year, brought immigrants pouring into the Mid-West, to Illinois, Wisconsin, Iowa and Missouri. For with the war over, rails were pushing west again. In its darkest days, Lincoln had found time to charter three new lines through the Mid-West to the booming mining territories of the far west. The California gold rush of 1849, which brought 100,000 people scrambling across the continent in one year, was followed a year later by the great Comstock strike in Nevada. The Comstock Lode, producing $25 million in gold and silver a year, more or less financed the Union through the Civil War. Meanwhile stagecoaches followed the prospectors, rattling over the prairie of the Mid-West from fort to frontier fort, carrying mails and gold-dust between the new mining camps at Denver, Virginia City and Last Chance Gulch, and the Mid-West river-port railheads on the Mississippi and Missouri.

Moreover, a 30-year-old victualler named Philip Danforth Armour had set up a meat-packing house in Chicago in 1863 and made a fortune selling pork to the Union army. Armour was a prime mover in the building of the Chicago Union Stockyards, which opened on Christmas Day 1865, on a 345-acre tract south of the city where nine railways converged. On them cattle were shipped in for slaughter from all over the farming Mid-West, wherever rail had reached—St Louis, Kansas City, St Joe, Missouri, and Omaha.

Abilene was the first of the roaring Kansas cow towns in the Mid-West where these cattle were gathered for the railway to Chicago, with three hotels, ten saloons, ten boarding-houses and various private establishments where 'Calico Queens' from Kansas City and St Louis offered the comforts of home. Their wooden false fronts lined Texas Street, where Texan drovers would announce the end of their six-week trek across the Mid-West from Fort Worth by stampeding their bawling beasts through town with a volley of pistol shots and Rebel yells. Once their cattle were pastured outside the town, the cowboys were free to collect their pay and start spending it on haircuts, girls, whisky, new boots, and hats—usually decorated with Texas stars. Most were Confederate veterans; some had not yet worn out all their distinctive grey clothing. In liquor, they tended to refight their lost war. Shootings were frequent. The leading citizens hastily built a jail and posted notices outside Mid-Western towns forbidding firearms within the city limits. The Texans cheerfully riddled them with bullet-holes and rode on, clanking. Finally, Abilene hired itself a sheriff—Wild Bill Hickock, who personified the first instance of a classic Western dilemma. The only way for his community of pacific Northern farmers to protect themselves against a floating population of defiant Southerners, descending armed and thirsty out of Indian territory, was to hire violence to fight violence. It seldom worked.

On the whole, the cowboys co-existed peaceably with the Cherokees, Kiowas and Osages whose territory they crossed on the way across the Mid-West from Texas to Kansas. The Indians collected ten cents toll per head on cattle driven over their land, and let their drovers pass. There was no reason for conflict. The cowboys followed their semi-domesticated herds as the Indians followed the buffalo, living on their meat, clothing and housing themselves in their skins. They shared the grass as fishermen share the sea. Their enemies were the railroads, bringing the buffalo-hunters and behind them the homesteaders who ate up the free range of the Mid-West.

Throughout the 1860s, small Indian wars flared up across the Mid-West. The bitterest was with the Sioux of the Dakotas, Montana and Wyoming, who in 1868 managed to block the building of roads into their reserves. In 1874 gold was found in the Mid-West at Deadwood in the Dakota Black Hills, and the rush of prospectors into Sioux territory, followed by the Northern Pacific railroad, provoked a second Sioux War. In 1876 a cavalry force was sent to reduce them. A group of 260, led by Lieutenant-Colonel George Custer, was cut off near the Little Big Horn river on Sunday, 26 June, and massacred to a man.

SUMMARY TEN

The following passage is taken from a discussion between a doctor, a lawyer, and a sociologist on whether capital punishment should be re-introduced in England or not.

Using only the information given in the passage, write a summary consisting of *two* paragraphs:

a the arguments for re-introducing capital punishment, *and*

b the arguments against re-introducing capital punishment

Do not try to summarise everything in the passage, but select from it the material needed for your paragraphs. These should be written in clear, concise English, *and as far as possible in your own words,* although you may retain some words and brief expressions which cannot be accurately or economically replaced.

Your whole summary should not exceed 160 words altogether, and at the end you must state the number of words used.

Doctor First, I ought to say that some crime is caused by disease. A few murderers cannot help themselves because of the condition of their minds and it seems unfair to execute the sick—especially those who are desperately ill. Society has a duty to look after them and, if possible, to cure them. We don't execute drivers who are alcoholics even though their actions may kill others; we try to rehabilitate them.

Lawyer Yes, but society has to be protected from those whose actions undermine it, whether they are lunatics or not. To put someone in prison for life is not the best way to cure a madman but society has the right to feel secure from his attentions. At a time, too, when there is not enough money to go round for new schools, hospitals, and old people's welfare it seems hard to have to use our scarce resources in keeping a criminal under lock and key. In any case, the law protects those who are so sick that they are not responsible for their actions. When capital punishment was on the statute book madmen were not executed.

Sociologist We really need to examine what the forces are which lead people to murder others. A murderer need not be mad but may be pressurised by social forces to such an extent—poverty, bad housing, frustrated education, the inability to progress in society—that he is driven to violence. Capital punishment may satisfy primitive desires for revenge but it attempts to treat the symptom and not the disease.

Doctor There is a serious moral, or even religious, argument against capital punishment. What right has any man to take the life of another?

Sociologist Well, the state assumes it has the right to take life in time of war in order to maintain one social system or impose another. But war is barbarous and so is capital punishment.

Lawyer And so is murder, of course. Perhaps the death sentence should be retained for the murder of policemen, prison warders, or court officials on official duty. They come into close contact with violent men and need extra protection.

Sociologist I cannot see why they should be singled out. What about security men, night-watchmen, and ordinary users of the highways? They need protection, too. Violence wielded by the state will beget violence.

Doctor Perhaps the only justification for re-introducing this form of punishment is that it deters others and makes would-be criminals think twice.

Lawyer I doubt whether that could be proved. The incidence of murder and violent crime does not rise significantly on the abolition of capital punishment in a state.

Sociologist What happens if you chance to execute the wrong man? If you have put him in prison he can be hauled out and be given a pardon but death is for ever.

SUMMARY ELEVEN

The following passage is taken from a report on value for money in clothes.

Using only the information given in the passage, write a summary consisting of *two* paragraphs:

a how the testers ensured fairness in their tests of the little black dresses, *and*

b why the judges at the end of this report (not given here) should decide that the £6 dress was the best value for money

Do not try to summarise everything in the passage, but select from it the material needed for your paragraphs. These should be written in clear, concise English, *and as far as possible in your own words,* although you may retain some words and brief expressions which cannot be accurately or economically replaced.

Your whole summary should not exceed 150 words altogether, and at the end you must state the number of words used.

Could you say that never, at any time, did you long for a dress by one of the great designers? Did you believe that you would look far more attractive if you could afford to buy clothes in Paris?

We wanted to find out what one of these couture dresses would do for ordinary people. We could not carry out a full scale test, obviously, on all the fashion houses' dresses, compared with all the other kinds of dress, at other prices, one can buy. What we could do was to get one example of a couture dress, two or three others at different prices, put each of them on several young women, parade them in front of fashion experts (and a few non-experts) and challenge them to tell us which was the high-price dress. If they all picked it out without difficulty, then it might be a good idea to start saving up. If they didn't, we could relax in the clothes we can afford.

To make the comparison as simple as possible, we chose the 'little black dress' to which fashion journalists are devoted. The first was an original model from one of the great fashion houses, made up to order—£66. The second was fairly widely advertised but was not a household name, on the expensive side—£17. The third was made by a well-known member of the Fashion House Group of London—£6. The fourth was from a well-known chain store, chosen as being very cheap—£2. Since we found that there was least choice in the most expensive range, we bought the £66 dress first, and chose the rest to be as like it as possible. The £66 dress was made of wool and silk, the other three of acetate and viscose rayon. The most expensive dress had one lining sewn in and another loose, the next most expensive had one, loose, lining. The other two dresses were unlined. All the dresses fitted someone whose measurements were a standard size 14.

The wearers

To wear the dresses we chose four women who wore size 14. Their heights varied from 5 ft 3 in to 5 ft 8½ in and their weights from 8 st 4 lb to 9 st 10 lb. They were a cross-section of women likely to wear the dresses (as distinct from models chosen by fashion houses to display their clothes to advantage). We described the dresses to the wearers and left them to bring what jewellery, shoes, etc., they thought suitable.

The judgment

We chose a panel consisting of eleven people interested in clothes who were used to looking at them carefully and critically. Five were professionals—a fashion journalist, a lecturer in fashion, a fashion design consultant and two dress designers. The others were men and women specially interested in clothes. The 'models' paraded at a party—the natural habitat of the 'little black dress'—in front of the judges, each wearing each dress in turn. The panel assessed the general effect of each dress on each model, and how it fitted her. They were allowed to look closely at the dresses and study the texture and workmanship, but not examine the hems or inside seams (they were guests at a party).

What the Judges Thought

Fabric and finish

The judges liked the fabric of the £66 most. They liked the finishing of the £6 dress particularly, and thought it better than that of the couture dress. They thought the finishing of the other two dresses was less good.

Fit

This time the dress at £6 and the dearest at £66 came out as fitting differently shaped but officially the same sized people almost equally well. The cheapest at £2 came next, and the one which cost £17 quite a long way behind.

General effect

The dress costing £6 was judged the best for general effect and appearance on all four wearers. Next best was the couture dress at £66 followed by the cheapest. The one which cost £17 was quite a long way behind.

Guessing the price

This was something the panel found very difficult. Estimates for the dress which cost £2 varied between £3 and £6, for the £6 between £4 and £60 (though most were in the £12 to £20 range); all the estimates for the £17 dress were from £5 to £10 and for the dress which cost £66 they varied between £9 and £45, with most guesses around £15. The professional experts did no better than the rest of the panel at price guessing.

SUMMARY TWELVE

The following passage is taken from an examination of the value of advertising.

Using only the information given in the passage, write a summary consisting of *two* paragraphs:

a the contribution made to our daily lives by advertising, *and*

b the arguments offered against advertising

Do not try to summarise everything in the passage, but select from it the material needed for your paragraphs. These should be written in clear, concise English, *and as far as possible in your own words,* although you may retain some words and brief expressions which cannot be accurately or economically replaced.

Your whole summary should not exceed 160 words altogether, and at the end you must state the number of words used.

The advertiser's chief concern is to sell. To do this he does not mind how much he distorts or suppresses the truth. The public is in such a state of confusion owing to the multifarious and conflicting claims of advertisers that it is genuinely baffled and does not know which product to trust. In the days when a man could grow and make most of his necessities for life, advertising was certainly not important, but the changing times have made it difficult for every man or woman to evaluate every product individually. Advertisers claim to give information so that the public can make up its own mind. Time can be saved by knowing what is available and where it can be bought. From a newspaper or from television the public can be shown what is on the market. The choice is increased rather than restricted by advertising.

Although the law does not allow products to make false claims for themselves and gives the consumer the right to expect in full what is offered by a manufacturer in his advertisements, the techniques of the salesmen remain subtle. Needs are invented in order that they may be satisfied. Fears which are often secret, jealousies, envy, the desire to be attractive to the opposite sex, may all be exploited by those who wish to sell their products.

Some advertisements have literary merit or contain material of aesthetic appeal. The standard of photography, background music, and language can be high but usually in order to appeal to the widest public some sales material deliberately lowers the value of language. Clarity of thought is often undesirable so far as the salesman is concerned; he prefers to cloud reaction with emotion and prejudice. By careful selection and omission he can achieve the effect at which he is aiming.

Advertisements certainly display much humour and colour; they are often entertaining, and drab surroundings are given interest by bright, eye-catching posters. They are particularly appealing when they use photographs or, on film or television, shots of far-off magical places. Commercial radio and television are able to survive and offer the public good entertainment only because they are financed by the companies that buy advertising time on their channels. It is an accepted fact that national and local newspapers would not exist without the support of the revenue they receive from advertising.

Nevertheless, the ugliness of the hoardings and the space lost in publications to advertising are irritating features of daily life. The interruptions to radio and television programmes in order to allow a manufacturer to bombard the public with the merits of his product cheapen rather than enrich our daily lives. Large sales, however, mean that products can be manufactured cheaply in bulk so that the consumer himself profits from advertising through lower retail prices. Competition in commerce, from the manufacturer right down to the retailer, must ultimately benefit the housewife as she does her shopping . . . and advertising encourages such competition.

SUMMARY THIRTEEN

The following passage is taken from an article on Britain's footpaths.

Using only the information given in the passage, write a summary consisting of *three* paragraphs:

a ways of establishing and maintaining rights of way, *and*

b the dangers that threaten footpaths, *and*

c the advantages of using footpaths

Do not try to summarise everything in the passage, but select from it the material needed for your paragraphs. These should be written in clear, concise English, *and as far as possible in your own words,* although you may retain some words and brief expressions which cannot be accurately or economically replaced.

Your whole summary should not exceed 150 words altogether, and at the end you must state the number of words used.

Custom and usage are accepted as methods of establishing a right of way. Our ancestors simply took the most convenient route to a local meeting place or the next community, skirting a swamp here, a wood there, and crossing a stream at a suitable place. Now section 34 of the 1959 Highways Act defines a period of twenty years' undisputed use of a path over freehold land as sufficient proof that it has been 'dedicated' to the public.

Other paths have been established by statute. It might have been a condition of enclosure that a right of way be granted or paths can be established by agreement between the local authority and the landowner. Local authorities also have powers to create footpaths compulsorily.

Some paths appear, however, to have outlived their purpose and have not been used for a very long time. Many have become overgrown and obstructed, often deliberately. There have been frequent complaints about inadequate signposting and publicity.

Ploughing-up has especially caused concern. A farmer who wishes to plough the whole of a field across which a footpath runs is required to give notice of his intention to do so to the highway authority not less than seven days before the operations are due to begin. Then, within six weeks after ploughing has been completed, he is required to restore the footpath.

These provisions have often been ignored and some farmers have sought to deter people from using footpaths by 'Trespassers will be prosecuted' and 'Beware of the bull' notices. The former has no legal validity and pasturing a bull over twelve months old in a field where a footpath runs is illegal in most areas.

Rights of way have been built over and sometimes lost for ever. Developers are required to apply for an order from a magistrates' court to divert or stop up a highway.

There is now a growing desire to 'get away from it all' as motor cars force walkers off the roads. Many country lanes have become thoroughfares and there is little pleasure to be had in walking when you have to scramble on to a verge every few minutes. Footpaths provide an escape: no cars to pester you, no noise or fumes, and only the good country smells. Motorists flee from the stress of the roads to stride out at ease across country.

Mapping is one way of seeing that footpaths are used. It also ensures that they are not interfered with. It is fun to plan a ramble and with the help of a map to explore; there is a sense of satisfaction in finding one's way with a compass and a chart. It is good to know that one is part of history, treading the same soil as our ancestors.

SUMMARY FOURTEEN

The following passage is taken from an article on Cornwall by Colin Wilson.

Using only the information given in the passage, write a summary consisting of *two* paragraphs:

a the reasons why people go to Cornwall for their holidays, *and*

b the ways in which Cornwall is being spoiled

Do not try to summarise everything in the passage, but select from it the material needed for your paragraphs. These should be written in clear, concise English, *and as far as possible in your own words,* although you may retain some words and brief expressions which cannot be accurately or economically replaced.

Your whole summary should not exceed 150 words altogether, and at the end you must state the number of words used.

Incompetent commercialisation is destroying places like Cornwall. I moved here nearly ten years ago because I thought it was one of the most peaceful and attractive counties in England. Since then I have watched it changing into a poor imitation of Blackpool. And I have heard the locals put the blame on financial sharks from London, and then seen these same locals apply for permission to cover the cliffs with grey, box-like bungalows. They explain their change of policy by declaring that 'it's got to come anyway'.

But has it? This argument fails to recognise that the crowds who now come to Cornwall—and the Lake District and the Scottish Highlands and the rest of Britain's 'unspoiled' beauty spots—are *escaping* from Blackpool and Brighton.

I made this interesting discovery three years ago, when I went to visit a friend in Blackpool in the height of the holiday season. The beaches and promenades seemed as crowded as one would expect, but I was struck by the number of 'Vacancies' notices outside guest-houses. My friend confirmed the suspicion: that the Blackpool regulars have discovered the existence of the Northern Highlands and the West Country.

In Cornwall, for many years, the season has been starting earlier and finishing later. The first result, of course, was a splendid rise in prosperity. An ex-Soho friend of mine set up a market stall on the quay to sell imitation jewellery at two shillings a time. Within two years, he had made enough money to buy a large building on the quay and turn it into a small Woolworths.

But now comes the problem. Car parks are needed, hotels, amusement arcades, gift shops, reasonably cheap cafés. A percentage of the visitors like the place and decide to settle here, so that every spare field with a view of the sea becomes the site for a dozen bungalows. To some extent, these needs can be satisfied; there is room for expansion. But when this is exhausted, the real problems arise. Cornish lanes are narrow, with high banks; they were never intended for heavy traffic. Cornish fishing villages tend to be surrounded by a circle of steep hills, so there is only limited room for car parks or hotels.

Since the crowds are escaping, it is hardly good sense to allow the development to proceed along such lines. Neither is it good sense to cover every foot of coastline which is not protected by the National Trust with suburban-type bungalows. The crowds are not here because they want amusement arcades on every quay, or stalls selling candy-floss and fish and chips on the beach.

No one seems to be quite sure what ought to be done. But the basic needs are surely clear enough. The increased flow of visitors to the remoter holiday spots is a sign of revulsion against urbanisation and mass entertainment. The problem of these remote spots is to cope with the increased flow while retaining the character that brings their popularity. This obviously cannot be done if the places themselves are perpetually choked with thousands of cars. Newquay used to be Cornwall's most popular holiday town, but it is now an ugly replica of any northern town, with a perpetual traffic jam from June until October. St Ives is moving in the same direction. It is time the locals applied a little common sense to the problem, before they kill the goose that lays the golden egg.

SUMMARY FIFTEEN

The following passage is taken from a report of the Conservation Society on the problem of over-population in the world.

Using only the information given in the passage, write a summary consisting of *two* paragraphs:

a the problems caused by the world's over-population, *and*

b the suggested solutions to the problems caused by the world's over-population

Do not try to summarise everything in the passage, but select from it the material needed for your paragraphs. These should be written in clear, concise English, *and as far as possible in your own words,* although you may retain some words and brief expressions which cannot be accurately or economically replaced.

Your whole summary should not exceed 150 words altogether, and at the end you must state the number of words used.

At present the world population of 3,600 million is increasing by 2 per cent (72 million) a year, but this overall figure conceals important differences between countries. The western industrial countries, with one-third of the world's population, have annual population growth rates of 0·5–1·0 per cent, and 25–30 per cent of their populations are under 15 years of age; the undeveloped countries, on the other hand, with two-thirds of the world population, have annual growth rates of 2–3 per cent, and 40–45 per cent of their populations under 15. Robert S. McNamara recently pointed out to the World Bank: 'If, by the year 2000, the developed countries were to reach the point at which couples replace themselves, and the developing countries were to reach that point by the year 2050, the world's present population of 3·5 billion would not become stationary before the year 2120, and would then stand at 15 billion.'

The problem of over-population must be tackled with the utmost determination. For the undeveloped countries this is a matter of life and death, and all usable help in communications and technology should be offered by the developed countries. At the same time, the developed countries should publicly accept the aim of stabilising their own populations, both as an example and because their citizens will, for some considerable time, go on consuming and polluting far more than those in the rest of the world.

The production and proper distribution of food will be a dominating problem for the undeveloped countries for many years. Help is needed from the developed countries to provide the safer (but more expensive and difficult) methods of pest control, and also to assist agricultural improvements in forms that do not destroy the existing social orders. This assistance should be tailored to the needs of the recipients rather than to the convenience of the donors.

Since the earth is finite, the long-continued growth of consumption of materials and energy is impossible, a truism which should be engraved on every economist's desk, if not on his heart. The continuation of Western extravagance alongside scarcity for the rest of the world appears neither morally justifiable nor likely to endure, unless the developed countries put themselves into a state of siege. The only alternative is for the western countries to reduce their demands on the earth as a source of raw materials somewhat earlier than they would be forced to do in any event. This will require basic changes in their economic systems, which are at present designed to give the maximum satisfaction of needs.

This is not a simple demand that we must 'lower our standard of living', since a change of the economy to reduce waste and pollution could lead to a marked increase in 'goods', such as a pleasanter environment, which do not appear in the national accounts book but are none the less real.

The report, *Resources and Man,* by the National Academy of Sciences, says 'It is our judgment that a human population less than the present one would offer the best hope for a comfortable living for our descendants, long duration for the species, and the preservation of a decent environment. Man must also look with equal urgency to his non-renewable resources—to mineral fuels, to metals, to chemicals, and to construction materials. Their overconsumption, or waste, for the temporary benefit of the few cannot be tolerated.'

Many things at present threatened by the upsurge of population are the heritage of all mankind: wild country and landscape, the varied and beautiful forms of life which enrich the earth, ancient cities, and the fragile human cultures which have not yet been absorbed. All are irreplaceable; but unless the richer nations combine to compensate these countries for leaving these things intact they cannot expect them to survive.

SUMMARY SIXTEEN

The following extract discussing the problems caused by cars in the cities has been taken from a series of interviews with car owners and former car owners.

Using only the information given in the extract, write a summary consisting of *two* paragraphs:

a the suggestions made for solving traffic congestion in towns and cities, *and*

b the reasons given by people for having cars of their own

Do not try to summarise everything in the passage, but select from it the material needed for your paragraphs. These should be written in clear, concise English, *and as far as possible in your own words,* although you may retain some words and brief expressions which cannot be accurately or economically replaced.

Your whole summary should not exceed 150 words altogether, and at the end you must state the number of words used.

'I would never give up driving completely—why should I?' said John Peyton, Minister for Transport Industries. 'Cars give people a much freer life—one doesn't want that freedom taken away.

'People are very selfish, they expect the road to themselves—no one has the same attitude to the pavement. To help combat this feeling people must be left in no doubt that the rules apply to them, and not just to others.

'One must appeal to people's better nature,' he continued, 'and encourage them to limit the use of their car.

'One can easily make blank regulations from the Ministry prohibiting cars but I feel it is basically the responsibility of the local authority who know local conditions to create pedestrian precincts, bus lanes, etc.'

Freedom to go anywhere at any time is something that appeals to Alisdair Aird, editor of *Motoring Which?* Driving into the Consumers Association's offices in Charing Cross saves him up to half an hour on his journey from Totteridge compared with using public transport.

'I really need someone to take the decision out of my hands,' he said. 'If the GLC stopped private cars going into the centre of town, I would be quite grateful to them.'

He has no mercy for car owners. 'I think it is important for them to pay for the road systems they demand in cities. For me the answer is a road-pricing system where a meter in every car would tot up according to the amount and area in which people drove. Quiet country lanes would be cheap and busy towns and cities expensive.'

Superintendent Raymond Coxon of Thames Valley Traffic Police thinks that people should park on the outskirts of a town and then pick up a bus service to take them into the centre. Then a town could take on a life of its own. People could move around without accidents.

'Persuading people to ration the use of their cars makes good sense only if public transport sufficiently improves to become a real alternative,' he said. 'Bus services need to be quick and inexpensive so that people can rely on them. People living in rural areas particularly could not do without cars: rail services are intermittent and in some cases non-existent.'

Chief Superintendent Coxon continued, 'I am as selfish as the next man. Driving my car—a Rover 2000—enhances my social life and means I can easily get to the theatre in London from my home near Oxford.'

Lady Dartmouth recently compiled a report for the United Nations on ways of creating a better environment. 'I do believe,' she said, 'in motorways and by-passes around towns so that towns and cities become more attractive places to live in.' She has the advantage of living in the centre of London yet still admits to using her car occasionally.

'I don't like driving, and only drive for convenience, never for pleasure. I would never completely give up because I wouldn't want to be helpless in that way.'

A person who has made the switch from car to bicycle is Sam Wanamaker, now director of the Southbank Globeside Trust. He is not completely happy about his decision. 'It's not easy giving up something that is so convenient,' he admitted. 'The main thing I miss is that when I was in a car I felt alone and anonymous. I used to use the car as a place where I could think about things quietly.' Would he ever buy another car? 'I don't know,' he replied, 'but it is significant that the bike my daughter bought me can be folded up and put into the boot of a car.'

SUMMARY SEVENTEEN

The following passage has been taken from a discussion about the future of village life.

Using only the information given in the passage, write a summary consisting of *two* paragraphs:

a the factors contributing to the decay of village life, *and*

b the factors which may contribute to the survival of village life

Do not try to summarise everything in the passage, but select from it the material needed for your paragraphs. These should be written in clear, concise English, *and as far as possible in your own words,* although you may retain some words and brief expressions which cannot be accurately or economically replaced.

Your whole summary should not exceed 160 words altogether, and at the end you must state the number of words used.

The best guarantee that there will be any real countryside left to enjoy by the year 2000 is the provision of a satisfying and reasonably prosperous life for those who depend on it for a livelihood. A flourishing agriculture is an obvious requirement, but with mechanisation reducing the demand for human labour, it becomes more and more important to see that other industries are encouraged to establish themselves in the countryside. If this is not done, many villages will decline. Rural depopulation is already serious in some areas, notably mid-Wales, parts of the West and North-west and East Anglia and in the Pennine region. Losses of over ten per cent are not infrequent. Agencies like the Rural Industries Bureau can do much to reverse this trend.

The purchase of second homes in the country by town-dwellers is another factor in off-setting population losses. It has led to the regeneration of thousands of cottages which would otherwise have crumbled away, but the contribution to the village which can be made by those who live there only at week-ends and holiday times is clearly limited.

Much more needs to be done to bring employment to country districts. If the 'country' aspects of town and country planning were given more weight, standards of living in the countryside might be raised appreciably. This refers, of course, not only to making life better with piped water and main drainage, the provision of power supplies and good communicating side-roads but also to enriching the quality of life itself, particularly in moments of leisure.

One aspect which causes much discontent in the villages is the decline in public transport. Between 1957 and 1967 the British Rail passenger network slumped from 14,622 miles to just under 10,000 miles and country areas were among the hardest hit. When closures occurred, angry villagers were promised that bus services would be introduced to replace them. This has not happened on anything like the scale required. Where services have been started they are often grossly inadequate and many more have already been stopped because they are 'uneconomic'. The result has been a vicious spiral of poor services and more cars on narrow roads; this last factor destroys the very peace and quietness of villages which the townsmen so admire. Moreover, rail cuts are apparently not at an end yet. It is absurd to suggest that the nation cannot afford forty million pounds a year when it spends hundreds of millions on projects like that of Concorde.

As the old die and the young are attracted by the bright lights of the nearby towns, villages cease to live at night. The Women's Institutes and the Young Farmers' Clubs do much to keep alive the sense of community and as the stress and rush of town life develop many will wish to escape into the countryside, where they will expect to find the villages there waiting for them. If the nation wishes to keep its rural communities as valuable units contributing to the economic development of the people, particularly now that we have entered a strong agricultural community in the Common Market, it will need to invest in its farms and villages. Then England's green and pleasant land will remain for all to enjoy.

SUMMARY EIGHTEEN

The following extract is part of a conversation in which three fifth-formers were discussing sport.

Using only the information given in the extract, write a summary consisting of *two* paragraphs:

a the arguments used in favour of sport, *and*

b the arguments used against sport

Do not try to summarise everything in the passage, but select from it the material needed for your paragraphs. These should be written in clear, concise English, *and as far as possible in your own words,* although you may retain some words and brief expressions which cannot be accurately or economically replaced.

Your whole summary should not exceed 160 words altogether, and at the end you must state the number of words used.

Jane I think some sports are cruel and degrading. Take fox-hunting, for example, or snaring rabbits, or shooting pigeons or deer.

Mark Yes, but you are talking about blood-sports. There is nothing wrong with athletics. I'd rather be out on the games field keeping myself healthy than staying shut up here in a classroom. Playing games makes you fit and alert as well as building up your body; you have to keep on your toes all the time. Who was it that said the battle of Waterloo was won on the playing fields of Eton?

Clive This isn't Eton and who wants to win battles, anyway? I do think sportsmen can be selfish. I've seen a group of hunters smash down fences, gallop across fields where the wheat has just been sown, and even cut up lawns of private houses. They think only of themselves.

Mark Any damage they do they pay for, but I don't think sport makes anyone selfish. In order to play in a team you have to learn to work with others and co-operate with them. This must help you later on in life. In our football team, although some of us are individualists, anyone who won't join in as one of the rest is soon dropped.

Jane We waste far too much time on sport in this school. When we have exams not far away we need all the time we can get to study. Some people think that they come to school just to play games. Hockey and football are all right for relaxation but they are not our main purpose for being here. Mark and the others keen on games get it out of perspective and spend hours and hours on sport.

Clive We can't work all the time, Jane. I know that I'm much fresher to tackle some maths after I've been swimming than after working at geography all the afternoon. Physical relaxation leaves the mind free to work.

Mark Whose mind? Listen to him! Seriously, though, I agree with Clive. Even those who only watch sport find it helps them to keep sane—to unwind, if you like. There is something about being part of a crowd at a football match; you feel caught up with the others and it's better to be part of a great sports movement supporting Leeds United than belonging to a fanatical political movement—like the Nazis, for example.

Jane Sport merely creates hysteria so that people use violence and cause damage. Games cost the country enough as it is. Think of all the money spent on playing fields, football pools, and horse-racing. Then we haven't enough for the old-age pensioners, the homeless, and the hospitals. In any case, sport is dangerous.

Clive It's a pity that people have to bet on games. It can lead to corruption and rigging results, but I suppose it is part of human nature. If men didn't bet on horses they would bet on whether it would rain or not. As for the danger, I grant you the point. Boxing *is* dangerous and so is rugby; but so is crossing the road. Living itself is dangerous.

Jane You have to cross the road but you don't have to box or play rugby.

Mark I think sport can be graceful and even artistic—even boxing and rugby. There is something about watching skilled players. But if you don't fancy boxing or rugby, Jane, why don't you try dancing or tennis?

Jane The only good thing about sport is that it provides an excuse to get out into the open air but games are taken far too seriously for my liking and become ends in themselves.

SUMMARY NINETEEN

The following extract has been taken from an article for those beginning to assemble hi-fi equipment.

Using only the information given in the extract, write a summary consisting of *two* paragraphs:

a the equipment needed for the best hi-fi sound reproduction, *and*

b how to ensure that the best hi-fi equipment is obtained

Do not try to summarise everything in the passage, but select from it the material needed for your paragraphs. These should be written in clear, concise English, *and as far as possible in your own words,* although you may retain some words and brief expressions which cannot be accurately or economically replaced.

Your whole summary should not exceed 150 words altogether, and at the end you must state the number of words used.

What is a Hi-Fi set composed of?

1. *The cartridge or pick-up.* The sound starts with the pick-up or cartridge which traces the record groove by means of a needle or stylus. The cheapest type is the *ceramic* cartridge producing much greater volume than the more expensive *magnetic* cartridge which requires a correspondingly more sensitive amplifier to boost the sound. The sound given out by a ceramic cartridge is hard and metallic: excellent for blowing in youthful eardrums at a discothèque but not for the subtleties of listening to Beethoven's Pastoral Symphony. The first rule to follow is: make sure that the equipment you buy has a first-class magnetic cartridge.

Before buying, therefore, try to *listen* to the various cartridges. When you have decided which cartridge you want, make sure your chosen Hi-Fi set-up includes it. If you buy a ready-made unit, have one made up for you by the dealers, or make one up yourself. Every link in the Hi-Fi chain must be a strong one and nothing is more important than a first-class diamond stylus. The cheaper stylus types, metal, sapphire, etc., need changing more frequently and, even more important, tend to wear out the records sooner.

2. *The playing-arm.* The playing-arm allows the cartridge to track the record as freely as possible.
The things to look for are:

(*a*) the ability to take different makes of cartridge. Some arms will take only their own cartridge, thus limiting your choice.

(*b*) an arm-lifting device. Taking the arm off the record involves a risk of scratching the record and even snapping off the minute stylus. With an arm-lift (a small lever by the side of the arm) one can lower the stylus into any track of the record without fear of damage.

3. *The turntable.* With a poor quality turntable the problems are changes of speed, flutter and rumble. The easiest solution is to buy your turntable ready mounted in a plinth. It is not difficult to mount a turntable on a wood plinth but flutter and rumble problems do sometimes creep in from lack of proper setting of the arm or motor and are not always easy to correct. The main point to watch here is that there is room to mount the playing-arm of your choice, and that all the playing speeds you require are included. Some of the latest turntables do not carry a 78 speed, for example, which is essential if you have a collection of cherished vintage discs.

4. *The loudspeaker.* The only thing is to visit a Hi-Fi showroom and listen to as many as you can (preferably not trying to listen to too many at the same time, as after a while they will all begin to sound alike!). The main point to watch is whether it will match your room. Obviously it is highly inconvenient to install massive speakers in a small room. The result, with a powerful 50-watt amplifier, would be to vibrate the very floor even at half volume. Equally sad is the sight of a pair of bookshelf-speakers in a room like a hotel lobby that obviously needs the largest type of speakers. Generally speaking, the larger the speakers the better the sound response, especially in the bass end of the sound spectrum.

SUMMARY TWENTY

The following extract, discussing the raising of the school-leaving age to sixteen, has been taken from a selection of children's essays and comments on the subject.

Using only the information given in the extract, write a summary consisting of *two* **paragraphs**:

a the arguments for staying on at school for a further year, *and*

b the arguments against staying on at school for an extra year, *and*

Do not try to summarise everything in the passage, but select from it the material needed for your paragraphs. These should be written in clear, concise English, *and as far as possible in your own words,* although you may retain some words and brief expressions which cannot be accurately or economically replaced.

Your whole summary should not exceed 140 words altogether, and at the end you must state the number of words used.

Little Ilford School, London E12

I am staying on because if I was to leave school in summer I probably wouldn't find a job that I could do; if I stay on I will probably have a few CSE papers to show as evidence that I have a little intelligence. Nowadays, it is worth staying on because a few qualifications can get you through life, because most bosses like intelligent people to work for them.

In staying on at school I would like to achieve a good enough grade for every subject I take. I wouldn't like to stay on at school and waste my time. I want to try and try until I succeed. My aim and desire is to become a pathologist or a radiographer, something where I can be of help to people who need help.

Jennifer Steele

I do not wish to stay on at school because I feel it may be a waste of time staying on. I may not achieve anything by staying on and I may be missing my chance of jobs in the outside world. Teachers advised me to stay on, but about six weeks ago I decided to leave because of money. I can't get the money I need.

My ambition is to be an apprentice or have a good trade behind me. But as I go for jobs or go up to the youth employment I am beginning to have second thoughts about leaving school. This thought about not leaving

school is because I feel that without any CSE grades, I may lose my chance.
John Gibbs

Salterbeck Secondary School, Workington, Cumberland

I know I'm not bright but I'm not altogether daft and I think it's a good idea to raise the school-leaving age to 16. Why? Raising it gives me a chance to try to take my CSE. I didn't want to stay on but my mother would have made me, anyhow. I hate school, homework, and having lessons. I want to join the Royal Navy when I leave and this can help me in a job like engineering. But if I don't go in the Navy it's best to have my CSE to fall back on.
Raymond Dodd

I am all against raising the school-leaving age. What is it going to prove or solve? Some people just don't want to stay on and if they are going to be made to stay on and take exams which they couldn't care less about or haven't the brains to take, then they could, and probably would, distract others and stop them from getting a good grade.

Schools are going to become more and more rebellious places with pupils being made to stay on and take examinations which about half the pupils don't want to take.
Susan Dixon

Gillian Hanson also went to talk to children in schools, in clubs, in the streets

People want to be independent. You go out to work, earn your own money and do what you want with it. You don't have to go to your mother for money.
Margaret, 15, Cambridge

Those without qualifications feel cheated. They thought they were going to get out and get a job quickly but they can't now.
Michael, 13, London

Not many of the teachers have control over us now, so when children are forced to stay on they're going to act up more. The teachers are going to live in terror!
John, 15, Workington

I think the people who stay on till 16 will be more sensible and grown-up.
Jennifer, 14, Kirkby

ACKNOWLEDGMENTS

For permission to use and in some cases slightly edit or adapt copyright material grateful thanks are due to the following:

Messrs B. T. Batsford Ltd for an extract from *Children* by David Kennedy; Messrs John Farquharson Ltd for an extract from *The Restless Generation* by Patrick Rivers, published by Davis-Poynter Ltd; Mr H. F. Wallis and Messrs Charles Knight and Co Ltd for three extracts from *The New Battle of Britain* (published 1972); Mr Jeremy Tunstall and Messrs Routledge and Kegan Paul Ltd for an extract from *Old and Alone*; *The Sunday Times* for extracts from the following articles—'The Reluctant Fifth' by G. Hanson, 'What makes a flu virus sick?' by I. Osman and an article by P. Gillman; The Conservation Society for an extract from their report on the United Nations Conference on the Human Environment 1972; *The Observer* for extracts from the following articles—'Cowboy Kingdom' by Ronald Bryden, 'The question is: would you give up your car?' by A. Levin, 'The magic of comics' by J. Gross and 'Was Mozart murdered?' by G. Unger-Hamilton; *Barclaycard Magazine* for an extract from 'The brighter world of hi-fi sound' by G. Davis; Messrs Bolt and Watson for an extract from the article 'The Incompetent Exploiters' by Colin Wilson (published in the *Daily Telegraph Magazine*); the Consumers' Association for an extract from the article 'The Little Black Dress' published in the January 1965 issue of *Which?*.